Stepstones

Compilation 2:
THE FREEDOM MOVEMENT

Excerpts from Readings Given to An
Al Miner & Lama Sing
Study Group

Stepstones – Compilation 2

By Al Miner and Lama Sing

Cover and book design by Susan Miner

Published in the United States of America

Library of Congress: 2018943018
ISBN: 978-1-941915-13-4

1. Lamasing   2. Psychic   3. Trance Channel 4. Freedom
I. Miner, Al   II. Lama Sing   III. Title

For books and products, further information, or to write Al Miner, visit http://www.lamasing.net

Freedom.
Freedom is that state of Knowing wherefrom
there are NO boundaries, NO limits, NO definitions,
save those which are <u>willfully</u> chosen.

– Lama Sing

The intent of this book is to provide a collection of excerpts to flip through for contemplation and meditation. They are taken from readings given for the Al Miner/Lama Sing Study Group on the topic of "Ultimate Freedom."

These readings have emphasized that this is a living work, brought to us in this time of great change for our world: For those who are seeking to awaken to the Truth of their Being, we are at the apex of a profound opportunity during this time of heightened Consciousness and change. Therefore, this book is also for you who are awakening. Join us. We welcome you.

We are Disciples of Freedom

Notes:

Christ/the Master – "The Christ is a Principle. It is a Spirit. It is the life. The Master has brought this Christ Consciousness into oneness with Himself. Thus, He has become the Christ. Just so many stumble over this." –Lama Sing

Father – When Al and this work employ the term Father there is no implication of gender, humanness, or religiosity whatsoever, but simply a word to refer to, call on, and address in a deeply personal way the God Source, the Creator of All, the Beloved. Al has said, "If it's good enough for Jesus, it's good enough for me."

Words – "It is important that all who might read these words understand emphatically we are using words to describe some event and actualities that have no corresponding words in Earth. So we are using the best that is at hand." –Lama Sing

The Channel – This name is used throughout the book to denote the difference between Al, the man in finite form, and the part of Al that has left his form and is in realms beyond to channel the information. It is capitalized when used in place of his name.

Lama Sing – This name refers to an individual Al has known and worked with beyond and in this and other lifetimes. It also refers to the group, others who join Lama Sing to participate in gathering and offering information from Universal Consciousness in the readings.

Form – While in "pure" Consciousness no physical-like form is present, in some circumstances, being expressed in a form that appears physical is joyful and/or useful, both to Al in his experiences as well as to communicate an understandable narrative.

In Earth – When referring to life on Earth Lama Sing uses the term "in Earth" because he is referring to Earth as a realm of expression, similar to the common use of "in heaven."

Understanding Freedom
Proposed to and Confirmed by Lama Sing

I would describe *Freedom* as that state in which the limitations of finite self, brought on by things such as guilt, sorrow, remorse, retribution, unworthiness, and habits that engender such, have been set aside with appreciation and compassion, fostering Love for Self and all life. I get this understanding from researching the readings on Freedom and habit, and also from experiences in prayers and meditation.

I would describe *Ultimate Freedom* as including these elements of Freedom, but adding to them: the ease to come and go on Earth without birth and death, to be conscious of and in dominion of being in more than one place or level of consciousness simultaneously, the unencumbered ability to communicate with any and all, and the freedom from anything that limits that has come to be the accepted norms of finiteness. I get this understanding of Utter Freedom from the descriptions and experiences of the Homeland Consciousness, where expression and experience, or creator and created, are totally Free, that brethren have been sustaining for us for eons, ever since they recognized that original intent as having gone awry in the Earth.

- Susan Miner

There is the prophecy which foretells that, if you shall *cleave* unto God and hold Him within as thy Way, thy Light, you shall find the Freedom from all limitation.

That work set before us all is that which can, if understood and accepted, Free the heart and the mind from the bondage of Earth and time and limitation.

Free the mind and the emotion, and you'll free the body from the present state of dis-ease.

One is given unlimited power when they have no personal need for same. *"Blessed are the meek and the humble of spirit for they shall inherit the earth."*

Freedom cannot be defined in mere words. It must be experienced and known; it must be claimed.

With Freedom comes all else.

With Freedom will come a faith so clear that it will empower you in all things, and you begin to know what it is like to walk as the Christ.

You *are* Free; the claiming of that Freedom is to unify the totality of your Being rather than having expression that appears, and seems, to function as separate.

To consider this topic of Freedom brings into the arena of contemplation all of the thinking and habit that conditionalize one's ability to *accept* Freedom.

Is it possible for one to claim True Freedom while dwelling in a finite realm? Yes. The answer is yes.

You cannot bind God's Freedom, which is given to you. You can *believe* it is bound, and because it is believed, there are the <u>experiences</u> of *feeling bound.*

One can free their consciousness, their spirit, their mind, yet, they will return to claim things which are a part of finiteness. Why? Because, for most, they have been chosen as, largely, the intent of the journey; for *some*, the intent of the journey is to become Free and to express that Freedom from within finiteness.

What are you willing to release in order to have Freedom? For, you cannot claim limitation and Freedom at the same time, can you?

Those who believed in finiteness and *death* (as you call it) had what they believed in seeing the Master on the cross "dying." They had no room in their consciousness for the awareness of what occurred; that the limitations of finiteness are not bindings upon them.

Those who know they can be Free have begun, taken the first step into, that Freedom. The knowing of it is the beginning.

Those who believe through the filters of limitation, the familiar, habit, are honored under their invocation of Universal Law: They have the right to be as they wish.

Those who wish to claim a journey in the manner in which they are pursuing it have that right; but those who claim Freedom and follow in the footsteps of the Master have their right [as well].

Truth is within. As you set this Truth Free, you begin to become it.

Would it be believed that there is a little Freedom over here and another little Freedom over there, and on and on, that one can be Free in this way but not that?

One who has claimed their Truth/their Freedom has claimed Themselves.

With Freedom comes knowledge, wisdom. It is like wiping a clouded window pane: That one can perceive not the pane but what is beyond it. See?

How do we measure the expression of Freedom?

There is no limit to Consciousness. There is no limit to Freedom.

See without the coverings such as, "Oh well, this is chance" or "Yes, but what about that?" These need to be swept away if one seeks to have the capital F Freedom.

You are, first and ever, a Child of God upon a journey of your choice.

The beginnings of Freedom are right there: by seeing what is and *Knowing* there is something beyond. See?

You are in the midst of a time that has the potential that you have sought for a considerable time, many of you for several lifetimes.

Those who realize that Freedom is their precious gift choose it and do not waver in their choice.

You, Sushannah, have chosen to be here to show that you *can awaken* within this lifetime, this journey in finiteness.

Do not look to the right or left but look to the center of your Being. Look to that which is calling you from within.

This journey should be filled with the joyful expectancy of one who Knows they are a Child of God.

Freedom is a sweet pathway, one which lovingly blesses all things.

To broaden the path of your expression of Truth, what are you willing to release in order to do that?

Do not fall prey to making judgments upon yourself of what has or has not been done or accomplished, for these can, almost silently, be woven into a fabric of limitation. They can cloud the pane of Truth that is You.

Be gentle and loving with yourself. Have a care not to judge the Truth of your pathway and your good works based upon the outer.

This is a time that calls to the Consciousness of those who are seeking.

The choices of some Children of God carry them into definition that is believed and loved and, thus, it *is,* and it becomes that which confines them.

The confinement engaged in builds understanding of the depth and breadth of Freedom.

Freedom is not an illusive quality to be sought after. It is already preserved within each soul.

Freedom is the nature involved in making choices.

When a choice is made based upon conditioned response, the freedom involved is relative to the confines wherein that daughter or son of God might be found.

You have absolute – *absolute* – authority over self. Bringing this to the forefront of your consciousness is your choice.

Do not allow yourself to begin the process of equating how well you are doing. These have value but not here, for to do so is to affirm separateness.

Believe in your power and rest in the Authority in believing.

Find the goodness, the peace, the joy, the freedom and act in accordance with same.

If you meet Darkness with Light, then let the Light be strong and pure, unwavering, not malleable.

In recent times, many souls were shown a pathway to Freedom. As they departed the realms of darkness, illusion, dominance, they came forth to bear the fruits of what had been given to them. Many of these now move along the path of Light to you to serve with you.

It is not only your deeds that create but the power of your words and thoughts. Give them the gift of the Christ's Grace.

Absolute Freedom is not an illusive quality to be sought after. It is already preserved within each soul.

Finding the full Knowing of Freedom from within an experience of definition becomes challenging; your *choice* limits the concept, the believability, of your True Nature.

In Utter Freedom, form would not be a part of the totality of Freedom. It would be a *choice* made *from* Freedom.

It is possible to attain Utter Freedom while yet in physical form if one believes. What would you do with that Freedom?

You would love, *utterly*, the realm of Earth if you were totally Free. You would love every aspect of it. You would see no good and bad, only the beauty of the opportunity, from Utter Freedom, to willingly express the choice to experience.

Would there be the ability of a group to be united in what they believe to be Freedom? First, there must be the Freedom of self, is it not so?

Can a group, if it agrees to a common singular intent, achieve that intent? Yes. Can the *group* release any limitation or any love of any certain state of being?

All things in the Earth realm are interdependent. To break Free from this is no small issue because the multitudes love the realm.

You can attain Freedom, and when you reach the point of Utter Freedom, it is probable that you would choose not to violate the love of the choices of the others around you.

If a group reaches Total Freedom it is possible they can create an environment that can exist within the embrace of the realm of Earth yet not violate the love of others ... unlikely, yet possible.

Freedom ... If one loves a certain food, is it difficult to give up that food? Is it difficult to break a habit you have become fond of? If you love someone and they do not love you back, is there a difficulty in that? Freedom ...

What is love? Is love a state of being that flows freely to and fro, exchanged without qualification? Is love the same yesterday as it is today and will be tomorrow? Love is qualified in the Earth in many ways. If we qualify something, have we not limited it, defined it, bound it?

When Jesus walked the Earth, He honored the Earth. He made Himself one with all that was and is. He was able, through His Love and Grace, His Oneness with God, to unify with whatsoever was before Him, including the process called death. Because He is one with all, He saw death merely as a pathway to move to the next existence.

Utter Freedom is seen by many as only being attained after the transition from the finite body.

To have Utter Freedom yet choose to be manifest in the Earth in a lifetime in a physical body, that Freedom would love *all* that is and would honor it. One who is utterly Free may (underscore may) choose to honor the perpetuation of what is loved by the multitude.

Believe in what you intend as your goal. Your words, your deeds, your intentions, should be singularly focused upon that goal.

Whether or not Freedom is reached in the *Ultimate* sense while yet in finite form is within the choices, the hands, of those who seek it.

Within the confines of structure comes the feeling of familiarity, comfort, the ability to know through definition. Without these confines or structures, many would feel, quite literally, lost.

It is possible for Utter Freedom to coexist within the defined. But those who have attained Utter Freedom would do so by honoring the choices of those who have not claimed Freedom.

Freedom comes about through the gradual realization of the fruits of claiming same: conditions of dis-ease would begin to dissipate, hunger would begin to vanish as abundance becomes beautifully apparent, and so forth.

All that is being discussed here is for the awakening of Self. It is to set Self Free.

One who has an attitude of Loving Neutrality begins the process of releasing any aspects of lack of ease. They begin to dissolve old habits that are limiting to them. They begin to open themselves to receive the gifts of God.

Within the individual who is Awakened and claiming the Christ Consciousness of Self, there are no constructed aspects of self that can limit the power of prayer.

You will know when you've Freed yourself when you see *all* things in the perfection at the core of their Being.

The true Self is that Center of your being which is your life force, God's intent which is You.

If you do not recognize the Center of who You are, loving that Center because God has placed this here, it would be difficult for you to set yourself truly Free.

Freedom tastes like honey, smells like a fresh field full of flowers, feels like a bird lazily soaring in flight, sounds like the water singing to you as it trickles over rocks and stones. Freedom is like the unbridled energy pouring forth from a child.

Freedom is the love of everything.

Freedom is the spotlight that shines out to help you see that your intention is reachable and guides you along the path to its attainment.

True Freedom lies within you. It must pass through veils of separateness, judgment, habit, fear, and so forth, like mutations on the beauty of who and what you are.

When you can repeatedly look at yourself in the looking glass and state, *I am a beautiful Child of God, uniquely created out of God's Love for me. I love You,* and it flows in genuine truth, you are setting yourself Free.

To truly love Self, go within, seek out the Center and allow yourself to feel It and know It.

Thought-forms of limitation in the world around you are mutations on the Truth.

When you have set yourself Free, you will see the collage of choices and know the beauty of the creative potential of God that has given these Children the right to create and to manifest this creation.

Are you *doing* something when you pause and intend something? When you go to your sacred place? It is good to affirm, "I *do* this in God's Name." Then, you and God are one in the doing.

Authority is the power that unleashes all of the beauty of your Uniqueness. It is the Authority to claim mastery over each limitation you might find.

Use your Authority with the loving Compassion of the Christ, and that Compassion will expand from the Center of your Being like radiating beams of a rainbow reaching out to touch the next energy and the next.

Remember Oneness: What is done to one impacts all; what is done to many impacts all with greater force.

The question was asked how to see events that are extremely challenging such as racism or cruelty. See as God sees: These are His Children journeying in the depths of experiences, brothers and sisters struggling to find themselves.

See beyond that which is at the forefront, beyond the sheathing.

Make a distinction between choices and choosing versus judgment. You make choices about what to eat, what to wear, where to go, and so forth. Those are not the same as judgment.

Judgment of another or of a state of being draws from the wellspring of self, placing the life energy in line with that judgment.

All who have attached a judgment in the past are nourishing that judgment. For that to conclude, there must be the realization, then, the *freeing* of the judgment, just as you would free a creature you have penned.

When you free your judgment, not only do you get your good energy back, but the thing that was being judged is unburdened.

In the face of challenge, *Know* the Truth.

In the power of Faith, many things can be wrought; in the power of Faith by one who has claimed the Christ Consciousness within, *anything* can be wrought.

In the Knowing, comes the Awakening. In the Awakening, the Faith is called to the forefront. Then, all else is placed in abeyance, and the Faith becomes the Light, the Power, the Force, that goes before.

By loving self – casting out judgments of self, freeing limitations and setting self Free – you do this for God within you.

As you pray for those who have lost their way, offering your Light flowing from the Center of You within, the Christ will take your hand and walk with you to touch them.

You are His, and He is yours. In your words, in your thoughts, in your deeds, every step that you take, remember this and the way will open for you.

You are God's miracle.

It is upon the wings of God's Love that we can all journey forth unto that which is calling to us.

God's Love is ever present within us. Knowing this, we become the channels through which God gives it.

Whenever you see anger, betrayal, acts of war, of violence, if you contribute like in kind to those, the result is the strengthening of that energy.

When you see those who do not act in accordance with the Law of God in following their free will choice, and you know these choices to be against thee and against that which is the known righteousness that you hold within, can you offer them God's Love? Or will you send them energy that will bind them, that will sheathe them in the guilt and sorrow of their deeds that they cannot know and see the Light of God within when this journey in which they have wronged another is concluded?

Find great joy in the peace and beauty of Pure Being.

We heard an outcry from some in the shadows who received the Love of the Christ and cried out that they were unworthy. What is the nature of one who is lost? Who has burdened them so, that they feel unworthy? From whence cometh the energies that surround them and sheathe them with the illusion of unworthiness? Who would cast such a thought to a brother or sister? Who?

Do not be at a distance sending hatred or anger, for you open yourself to *receive* those energies upon that same pathway.

All live within the body of God. What, in the body of God, would you ever hold anything but Love for?

You are not an idle, biological evolution. You are the intent of God to *Be* you.

You are gifted with the greatest of all gifts: the simple right of choice. Your Authority is the power that enables you to exercise that choice.

Love your bodies as Jesus loved the temple and acted to cast out that which would defile the temple; not with violence, but with deliberateness and love.

Never let your heart be weary in the face of that which is of finiteness. Rather, fill your heart with the Knowing that He dwells therein with you. He is that Loving Force that will lift you up whensoever there is the need. You have only but to ask and to open yourself.

Understand that True freedom cannot be based upon the outer. True Freedom is an inner attainment. When you are Free within the outer will follow.

Spirit is the pattern of the true beauty of the soul. It is the creation of God.

Do not shy away from that which seeks to claim you in habit. These are no more than items of clothing worn on a journey. Lay them aside, for they have served their purpose. But you have begun a new journey, a journey of the uttermost potential of True Freedom. Lay aside the old garments now … *not later but now!*

In God's kindness and in His wisdom He has given to you a blessing: that is the Freedom of choice. You have Freedom of will. Each of you has the Freedom to choose your pathways and your experiences.

You are beyond definition, even beyond explanation.

Within the Christ is our Father. Who is within you, if not the same?

Begin each day with the *Knowing* that it is a gift.

The day and the energies therein are yours. *You* decide whether they are a blessing or nay by what you carry away in that day's ending.

Pause before slumber and gather the harvest of the day just concluding and celebrate each aspect of the harvest. You are the master of the harvest.

The Peace of God is yours, for you are His.

Believe in that which comes to you in the realization that, as you have opened yourself, when the energy seeks to fill you, it is God's intent to fill you that you might be that full cup from which you can give to others.

You are facing an opportunity to not only set yourselves Free – not being bound to the limitations so familiar – but to contribute to the overall consciousness of your realm, which has a domino effect upon associated realms, including those realms unto which entities journey upon departure through the process you call death.

Cast aside the structure. You are an instrument of God without boundary.

All the energy centers are involved in the progression of one's consciousness, but this has to do with the interaction of the centers with the finite expression and the Spirit as it is involved with that finite expression. The Consciousness of Self has no such limitation.

There must be an inner joy, the state of Knowing that you are ever One with your Creator. In this, there will come that realization that the outer is the product of the inner belief.

Believe in your nature as an eternal Child of God and find joy in the moment, and the moment that follows will produce a result after its kind.

Do not struggle against burdens, for this gives them energy.

There is no burden outwardly that cannot be found internally as some neglect, some sense of ignoring the True Nature of your Being.

Your ultimate goal will be the emergence, the unification, of the spiritual with the physical, where no barriers stand between you in physical and in spiritual.

Recognize yourself as part of all that is … *everything*.

The Freeing of yourself – that you set aside habit that is limiting and hold joy within – is like opening the door to the chamber within you wherein God is. Your joy makes it possible.

For you to have true Freedom, would you expect to hold onto a single limitation? Freedom means that all things about you, within you, are Freed. The moment you reach that point of Absolute Freedom, all is yours.

As you are willing to give all things their Freedom, all things wish to be one with you.

Your inner Freedom must – see, *must* – bear fruit without.

From Loving Neutrality, you can See and Know. If you do not have Loving Neutrality, you cannot tell whether your hand is opened or closed because the part of you that is not Lovingly Neutral will color that.

If you wish to color over the Truth, there are many energies available in the Earth that will nourish that wish.

Guilt, sin, sorrow, remorse are the opposite polarities of True Freedom.

Journeying into the Earth is a healing intent. Your healing is a part of the gift you give to the Earth.

You are an eternal Creation of God. Even as you know this, you also know that you are in a physical body. When there is the realization that the physical body is by choice and that it is in harmony with the structure of the realm in which it is expressed, you begin to realize the power that you have by knowing this.

When the choice is to seek Truth, you begin the process of Freeing yourself; when you are comfortable in that which is familiar or gives you boundaries, you are not seeking Truth.

It is possible to have no boundaries and yet be in finite form. Whether or not one wills this, chooses it, is up to the individual.

You are eternal Creations of God in a journey in finiteness. The true realization of this will set you Free, abolishing separateness.

Your work contributes to the mass-mind thought and the collective consciousness that surrounds the Earth.

Where you are at present is very significant, foretold by many in millennia past: that during this particular period there would be a window of opportunity that can be used by those seeking to set themselves Free and contribute that Consciousness to mass-mind thought.

While there is the experiencing of finiteness, the eternal Self that is always present. This is being awakened.

What lies ahead is in the hands and minds, hearts, and spirits of the Children of God incarnated in the Earth.

Honor those who, every day, give prayers to you by pausing to receive.

The Consciousness has to do with the acceptance of your Uniqueness and your Oneness with God.

Emotion and mind are the tools with which your soul extends its spirit to do works of understanding and service.

The most powerful force you have lies within you. It is the presence of your Creator, the Force that is within and about all that is.

Freedom is yours. It has no prerequisites, no mandates, no boundaries. Freedom is, for Freedom is, in truth, Father.

It is possible to move within Universal Law in a harmonious way, a Lovingly Neutral way, intending no thing, merely honoring and loving one another.

You can love things but not need them. The love for them is as the open-handed holding of a beautiful bird; the need for them is the clenching of that hand.

The Truth of Love is Freedom, *absolute* Freedom.

Everything within the creation of God interacts. Therefore, your actions, your thoughts, your words, your deeds all contribute to the energies that are in motion.

The Light of God is ever present. All throughout that which is, is the Light of God giving it existence, providing it the opportunity and right to be.

Those who have actively sought and, through their choices, have reached a level of Consciousness wherein they are essentially Free, their Freedom has enabled them the choice: depart from the physical body or continue their tenure in the Earth. These, then, would be benevolent souls in service to God to those who are seeking. They would be active participants in the works of prayer because they are, while yet in physical form, connected to Spirit and, as such, those requests that flow to Spirit are theirs to respond to with the power of Spirit, which is as to say, the Christ.

Claim the glory of God's Light within, that which is your very life.

Cast aside the illusion of any need. Open yourself to receive in the peaceful joy as a Child of God.

You are among those souls who have the opportunity to be awakened and yet remain in the environs of Earth.

Awakening does not come about in every instance by a great happening on the outer but by a gentle realization that grows from within to without.

Ever should there be held in the mind and heart in any journey the affirmation that God journeys with thee.

Let us oft pause to give a blessing of Peace to any and all who are struggling with that which is unknown, that which is challenging, and that which is seen in the present time only as a burden.

Rise up this day and go forth, never turning back to gather up the burdens of the past, always looking to the forefront to see the opportunities to give of the wellspring within. As you do, the greater will be given.

This opportunity, were you to see it from here, is most assuredly one you would not want to be idle in.

The righteousness is yours, as a Child of God, to answer the calls, and the Master stands beside you to so do. Do, then, as He would do. See? Do no less than this. Mark you: *Do no less than this.*

Think of the power of the Authority of a Child of God as the signet of Righteousness that is yours and claim your Heritage.

Carry your Authority with you in your prayers. If a call comes to you, answer it from that position of Authority.

Every single day of your life is a gift. As it begins, affirm it. Look to the expanse of it and do all things at the side of your Father. Do this by affirming it as you arise. Make it the first activity of your day. Make it the last activity of that day. And make it a joyful pause whensoever you can all throughout that day.

Christ, when He walked the Earth and was challenged, did not accept the challenge but blessed it. Do the same.

Never forget, the most powerful force you have at your command is prayer.

The power of your prayer, when you are Awakened, is as the Christ.

Meet opposition without giving it the energy it is seeking to perpetuate itself. Violence begets violence; love begets love.

Mind and Spirit are not in opposition. As mind goes about discovering itself, it will come to know that it is the instrument of Spirit. Mind and Spirit are one.

You are seeking to balance, not so much so good against evil but habit on the one polarity and Consciousness on the other.

There is no right or wrong.

Reach out in heart, mind, and Spirit before any word comes forth from your mouth. As you do this, see all in the Love you feel within and the way will open for you.

Each one who takes a step has taken that step for all others.

The Kingdom of God is before you. Do you wish to seek it? In the Law Universal, you must seek, you must believe. *You* must set yourself Free.

You have chosen your journey in your current incarnation *knowing* that this pathway would be offered to you. As you claim it, the power – yes, the *power* – will awaken for you.

It is a matter of realizing your uniqueness, realizing your Authority as a Child of God, and putting that into action in your thoughts, words, and deeds.

To be a part of the work at hand is merely to choose it. In the choosing, you open yourselves to receive.

Can you not in this very moment feel the wondrous Love stirring within you, making you feel something wonderful, something you have known for a long time and had no word to describe?

You are a precious Child of God. Your claiming of it illuminates you, and this illumination has no limit to its potential.

Freedom in the Ultimate sense while yet in finite form in the Earth is within the hands, of those who seek it.

The knowing of Freedom will cast rivulets of light unto the darkness of illusion, that others may take of this light. And it will bloom within them, and they will become a source that reaches out beyond them to another, and they to another, and again, and again.

Do not question too long the nature of Truth as you find it expressed without; do rely upon that Truth that is within you: the Knowing that you are His.

Reach within often. Pause. Ask. Listen. Claim the Peace. Dwell in the Silence. And Love yourselves.

Allow yourself to Know your Spirit. In the Knowing of your Spirit, you begin the Knowing of God.

Send before you the Word of God. As you so do, all will part before you.

Recognize subtle shifts, events occurring beyond the ordinary, awakenings in perception out of the ordinary for you. The realization of energy shifts makes many things possible that were, just a bit before, much more difficult.

Recognize the Uniqueness, the individuality, of *each* Child of God and hold a special love of that Uniqueness: a compassion that understands the aspects of growth that seem to be propelling each one towards a destination, known and unknown.

Know the inner chamber of Holiness, where we, as in the Beginning, are in the present.

Seek the answer to ourselves: that God so Loves us that we came into Being.

As we journey in the glory of the beauty before us, we look at those things that are as coverings of the beauty of some of our brethren. We grant them forgiveness in the Name of our Lord God, that they might forgive themselves for that which they have and have not perpetuated; that they will look about and set free any burdens they have or are imposing upon others, knowing that it is God within them that grants them the power of His healing Grace and forgiveness. And as this journey continues on past this good work we do together, let us ever recall that we have paused here in the journey to claim and to offer forgiveness unto all that is.

Wherever there has been a word that you have taken as an affront to self, look upon the giver of it, that one who has spoken it. Whether it has been appropriate or misguided, it is a burden to both of you for so long as it is held within. If you have an expectation of retribution, of penance, that is required of you or another to you, you are burdened.

Look upon *all* your brothers and sisters and see them as your Father sees them: beautiful, worthy of your love, as He loves them.

Seek ye not a temple constructed of the substance of illusion, but seek ye the permanent Light of the temple of God within you.

Some in the realm called Earth know not the Christ; others know of Him and question. Those of you who bear His mark – in other words, who hold a love for Him within your being with all that you are – celebrate them, believer and non-believer, alike. For when the journey in finiteness is complete, shall you not stand before the same God? Will you not receive the same opportunities to know the Truth of who *you* are?

Do not pray beseeching a distant God, but within the temple that is eternally within you, stand side by side with God. Truth shall always be, and ever is, within you.

In a city called New York, or Bombay, or Calcutta, or the tiny isle of Bermuda? Who, in all of these lands and so many more, shall hear the call and Awaken?

If the one next to you is celebrating, holding the expectation of the Promise, and you next to them are clinging to the past, it is better that you step back than be a limitation to one who is seeking to set themselves Free.

Your goal is the Freedom from bondage of mankind's limitations, the ability to soar on high with the beauteous animals of your skies, the ability to dive to thy ocean's depths with the animals therein dwelling, the ability to communicate with nature, and lastly, but most importantly, to communicate with thy brethren. This is all within your grasp.

Free yourself, that you and your Creator can celebrate the beauty of your Uniqueness and the Uniqueness of all of your brethren.

Look to the keys that have been given to you. They were not given idly. Use them. If you find in your day's activities that you are burdened and unable to make a space for time with God, use the keys that have been given to empower you to change this.

It is said that those who shall rise to the forefront, those who shall be seen in the Light of God's Love, are those who Free themselves to Know Him. (Do not take these words to mean you must abandon all and go to the wilderness and be in meditation and prayer.)

When it was asked of Jesus, He did not say to the one asking, "Come here. I will do this for you." He asked them to call forth the Presence of God within them with these words, *"Do you believe?"* Immediately, the Path is open, and the Father within the one seeking answers their call. Jesus is the reflection of God within the seeker. Jesus is the Son of God; the seeker is the son or daughter of God. As the seeker opens to ask, they are One.

Seeing yourself as limited is a part of the choice of a journey in finiteness. Therefore, the choice of Freedom must be as simple as choosing not to see it as limited.

You have been sent by the Christ as surely as His Disciples of old were sent forth. As you have set yourself Free – set the ideal, the intent, before you of Oneness with God and claimed the Love of God and the Love of your brethren with no boundary – you are His. And as you go forth in His Name, it shall come to pass in a time that is known by you and He alone that no thing shall be impossible for you in His Name.

Here, in the Consciousness of the All, there is only Love. The truth is that's all there is everywhere.

The wonderful gift of free will grants you the right to move into an experience of your creation along with the combined choices of others to experience the depth and breadth of all that is. The inference is that this is the prime quest. Is it?

Dwell in the moment, surrounded in the Love of God and in the profound choice to move into the Sacred Silence and claim the Peace through the pathway of Loving Neutrality.

Seeing yourself as limited is a part of the choice of a journey in finiteness. Therefore, the choice must be, you see, as simple as choosing not to see it as limited.

As the Light builds, these energies are Universal; those who use them for different purpose, under the Law, have the right to so do. Do not subscribe to their choice. Their intent to darken the Light of God's Love within you. Rather, let this shine forth all the brighter in the face of challenge, in the face of adversity.

As it is sought from you, give it, but only as you know this to be a joyful service to your Father that inspires your soul, your Spirit, in the joy of its doing.

Your dedication and your faith will bring to you the Awakening of your Knowing, of your Seeing. As this is accomplished, you will become Free.

Freedom is the right of choice, invoked by realizing you have the Authority to choose.

As you exercise the right of choice, place before this an intent summoned from the Center of your Being, where you and God are One.

Be Free in your interpretation, in your assessment, in your expectation, in your knowing. If you cling to this little facet here or that little-loved aspect there, then the balancing forces will surely focus on that, and your choice to cling to something limited may have the effect of limiting you.

See the River of Life as God's Love flowing to all that is and beyond. Life is the Love of God. The life within your body is God's Love for you.

The Consciousness of one who is Free is not *distracted*. In other words, the scope of comprehension doesn't have boundaries.

Some of you have conditions upon your Freedom, and that is a part of the process of truly setting yourself Free: There is believed to be a responsibility along the lines of love that some cannot conceive of releasing, and other responsibilities that are believed in, and so forth.

You direct the course of your journey. You could think, *My, what have I chosen here?* Or, you could be very astute and say, *My, what have I journeyed into*, and realize these to be the collective choices of others.

See all things in Loving Neutrality.

You are the master of the harvest.

Consciousness Sees and Knows in a state of Oneness.

The Freeing of yourself is to set aside habit that is limiting, and that you would think in terms of there being an ever-present potential within you.

True Freedom has no limitation.

You have the right to Be, to choose to break Free from the limitations woven into the mass-mind thought-form prevailing in the Earth.

It is a matter of *realizing* your Uniqueness.

For we to say you will hear and know the Promise at this certain juncture, under these certain conditions and so on, would be to minimize the Glory of what awaits you.

Why do not all the wars stop if the Promise is upon the Earth? Why does not dis-ease vanish? Why would there ever be anything similar to conflict, disagreement, emotional challenges such as anger or hatred and that sort? The simplistic answer is because it can be; the more complex answer is because some are still choosing it.

If you have Freedom, you are love, you are compassion, you are joy, you are grace, you are forgiveness, on and on.

Freedom means that Knowing, Seeing, Being are all states in which you have fluidity.

Since all of Consciousness is a part of the Freedom that you are, Father's Word forms into that which brings you joy, whether you round the bend and see a field of beautiful yellow flowers, or a body of water and a tail-dancing dolphin, or some beautiful tropical birds that sing and come to rest upon your arm.

Freedom is the *presence* of the Knowing that you are a Child of God.

Be ever vigilant for the shift within, the indication that you are Awakening, Knowing, and Seeing.

You have the Authority to *command* this body, this mind. For You are Spirit eternal intended to Be by God.

In those winds of change, the Ocean of Consciousness that swirls about you, the greater you claim the Knowing of your Self to be an eternal Creation of God, the greater is your potential over all those things that are about you in the physical and spiritual sense.

As you seek to be in the presence of God's Grace, then be in the state of Peaceful Joy, for this is the expression of God and the balance point.

There are many nooks and crannies in the machinations that take place in the mind and the emotional pool of Earth. One can delve in these and swim about in the pool of emotion and thought literally for years. Or you can realize who You are, what You are, in this moment.

The Promise means that you love and have joy, sufficient that you open the Way. And it is that straightforward.

The strength of faith in each of you has endowed you with an environment of beautiful Light and Peace. It is this Light and Peace that we encourage you to claim, to recognize, to send forth in all directions, all ways, for you are opening the way with this, flowing from within you.

So many find difficulty in accepting Complete Freedom. For one reason or another – they feel unworthy, they feel guilty, they feel some sense of longing for something that is outside of Complete Freedom – and so they journey to a half-way point wherein they can satiate those desires, needs, whatever you would call them, until they are Complete.

Those who *choose* Freedom will, for the most part, choose to be disciples of that Freedom; not in a way that is invasive, but in a way that is demonstrative of the pure Love and Light of God within that gives Existence its potential, its Being.

Each individual projects himself into an image which is as a mask. This image can be cast aside, that the true Oneness and beauty of God's presence within can manifest. You are seeing the disengagement of your True Being from the mask you have created for yourself over your existence.

These are those times as have been prophesied: the call for the Faithful to join around and strong and faithful.

When one seeks to become free in the total sense of Freedom, it is not because they are denying something, choosing to abandon someone or others, individuals or groups; or even that they are, in a sense, casting a judgment upon the finite realms of definition.

Freedom is the giving up of those things which bind, quite straight forwardly, that you can Know Yourself in the completeness as God knows You in the moment of Him calling You forth to awaken from within His Being. It is that Knowing that sets you Free.

Being at One with God in all things brings a joyful heart to bear in all things. For the presence of your Freedom is a source of gladness to all whom you will encounter. And you will see, they react to this gladness they see in gentle and tranquil ways and reach out to interact with something they may not fully understand. But they feel it. And it is this opening of their feeling that allows you to give them a Line of Light to the Holy Spirit.

We would reiterate, just once more, the quest for Freedom is your holy right. For you *will* come to a point at some juncture in your journeys throughout the varying expressions of Consciousness where you will see Freedom for what it is: *You will know it to be the Glory of God that bears your name.*

❦

What Will (Most Likely) Be

A point of transition will occur. Those who prefer to continue on as they are and those who answer the Call will face one another. Some will bring this choice to a point of confrontation that may invoke an upheaval that will be felt from the Earth itself, *and* there will be the beauty of those dwelling in the same way but in a sense of peacefulness.

The movement will carry those who choose the Promise to a new realm of expression wherein no one is bound and where all will be Free to explore, to create.

That which is left behind through the choices of those individuals will stay in the energies of their habits they have collected over lifetimes. Those who remain will continue to have wonderful opportunities to discover the true nature of their being. And there is always the opportunity to move on through various means, one of them you call death and the movement into the Loving Neutrality of God, the River of Love and Light.

So, you would have a *realm* wherein many souls have "graduated" because they have set themselves Free from that which they have been dependent upon for many, many lifetimes because they now accept that they and God are One. And in the acceptance of this Oneness, they can be where God is, meaning wherever they choose. Some may choose to return now and then to bring the others a bit of the light of understanding, to bring a bit of hope, when one of their habits has burdened them too heavily. That is very, very profound because the gift that remains is like a flower that will never fade, its petals will never fall. It will remain, forever, a gift. Your dedication and your faith will bring to you the awakening of your Knowing, of your Seeing. As this is accomplished, you will become Free and become a light for others. Be ever vigilant for the shift within, for this will be the indication that you are Awakening.

The emphasis is only present if you are truly seeking; if you are not, well then, do these things if you wish and if not, that's just fine, and you will continue on the wheel of life… free to choose as you wish, free to be limited or unlimited as you choose or submit your choice to others. But look you carefully: Here is the time in the Earth that has been prophesied, and you have asked and it is being answered.

Know that God's Peace is ever yours.

୶୰ଡ଼

Oh, Lord, my God, I know that thou art with me now, as ever. In Thy presence do I claim my heritage as a living light, a spirit, formed now in the Earth to do Thy will and purpose.

That I might better accomplish this, help Thou me to see the beauty and uniqueness of my Being, to lovingly accept and manifest this to others, that that Spirit eternal might emerge with Its strength, love, compassion, and wisdom, to provide the tools for these works. I affirm this, Father, in mind, in body, and in spirit. So let it be. Amen.

———————

His peace we now offer to you all.
Celebrate yourselves
in the manner that you know we celebrate you:
without limit, without reservation,
without feelings of remorse
or that which has been.
Rise up upon all that has come before
and see yourself at the pinnacle of your decision
to be a True Child of God: which is as to say,
Free.

———————

Books by Al Miner & Lama Sing

The Chosen: *Back Story to the Essene Legacy*
The Promise: *Book I of The Essene Legacy*
The Awakening: *Book II of The Essene Legacy*
The Path: *Book III of The Essene Legacy*

In Realms Beyond: *Book I of The Peter Chronicles*
In Realms Beyond: *Study Guide*
Awakening Hope: *Book II of The Peter Chronicles*
Return to Earth: *Book III of the Peter Chronicles*

How to Prepare for The Journey:
      Vol I. Death, Dying, and Beyond
      Vol II. *The Sea of Faces*

Jesus: *Book I*
Jesus: *Book II*

The Course in Mastery

When Comes the Call
The Children's Story: Summary of When Comes the Call

Seed Thoughts
Seed Thoughts to Consciousness

Stepstones: Compilation 1
Stepstones: Compilation 2

For a comprehensive list of reading transcripts available,
visit the Lama Sing library at www.lamasing.net

About Al Miner

In 1973, a little more than twenty years after a near-death experience, a chance hypnosis session triggered Al's reconnection to the other side and began his tenure as the channel for the Lama Sing readings.

Since then, over 10,000 readings have been given in a trance state for groups and individuals from around the world, answering questions on a virtually unlimited array of topics. The precision of the information has been substantiated by individuals, professionals, and institutions. Those who have received personal readings continue to refer others to Al's work based on the accuracy and integrity of the information given.

Al has quietly served individuals and groups for over forty years, dedicating his life totally to this work. His focus now is research on Consciousness and its application in daily life. He currently has sixteen books in print.

www.ingramcontent.com/pod-product-compliance
Lightning Source LLC
Chambersburg PA
CBHW070642030426
42337CB00020B/4131